BUG BUILDERS

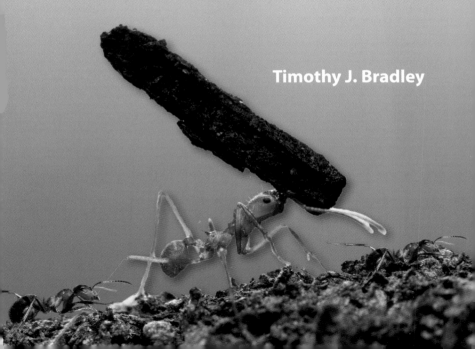

Timothy J. Bradley

Consultants

Timothy Rasinski, Ph.D.
Kent State University

Lori Oczkus
Literacy Consultant

Tejdeep Kochhar
High School Biology Teacher

Based on writing from
TIME For Kids. *TIME For Kids* and the *TIME For Kids* logo are registered trademarks of TIME Inc. Used under license.

Publishing Credits

Dona Herweck Rice, *Editor-in-Chief*
Lee Aucoin, *Creative Director*
Jamey Acosta, *Senior Editor*
Heidi Fiedler, *Editor*
Lexa Hoang, *Designer*
Stephanie Reid, *Photo Editor*
Rane Anderson, *Contributing Author*
Rachelle Cracchiolo, *M.S.Ed., Publisher*

Image Credits: pp.15, 32 Alamy; pp.18, 22 (background) Dreamstime; pp.13 (bottom), 16, 21 (top), 26, 27 (top), 39 (bottom) Getty Images; pp.12, 21 (bottom), 41 (right) iStockphoto; p.23 NASA; p.14 National Geographic Stock; pp.8 (left), 9 (bottom), 19 (top), 20 Photo Researchers, Inc.; pp.10–11, 38–39, 48 Timothy J. Bradley; p.35 Time Inc.; p.17 WENN.com/Newscom; p.7 (top) Newscom; All other images from Shutterstock.

Teacher Created Materials

5301 Oceanus Drive
Huntington Beach, CA 92649-1030
http://www.tcmpub.com

ISBN 978-1-4333-4821-1

TABLE OF CONTENTS

MAKING IT WORK

Engineers are people who find new ways to make things work. They build bridges. They dig tunnels. They make roads. They also plan how to build toys, forks, cars, and more! Some of the best engineers never went to college. They were born knowing how to build things. But these engineers aren't people—they are bugs!

Imagine a creature that can grow its own armor. What about a bug that can make silk that is stronger than steel? Insects can make structures as amazing as our biggest skyscrapers. Some use materials they find in nature. Others build things using their own bodies! These are not aliens from a science-fiction movie. These animal engineers build new things on Earth every day.

A spider builds a silk case for its eggs.

A wasp builds a hive.

THINK LINK

- Have you ever tried solving a problem by inventing something new?
- What needs do insects and people have in common?
- How do you think insects keep themselves safe?

BUG BUILDERS

Every animal needs to find ways to survive. All animals must search for food. All creatures must find safe places to live. Insects must avoid **predators**. But what exactly is an insect?

An insect breathes air. Its body is divided into three parts: head, thorax, and abdomen. It has three pairs of legs. And it has wings.

Insects are a type of **arthropod**. They have **exoskeletons** and jointed legs. Spiders are arthropods. Crabs and some sea creatures are, too. Around the world, these bug engineers have built small structures that help them survive in a big way.

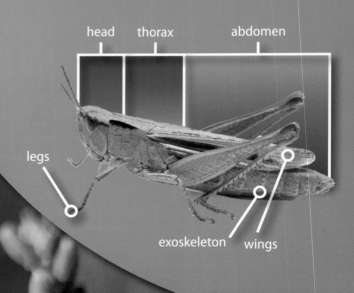

head   thorax   abdomen

legs

exoskeleton   wings

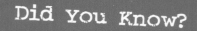

Did You Know?

In some cultures, fried and chocolate-covered insects, such as bees and ants, are considered a tasty treat.

a variety of insect snacks

Insects were some of the first creatures to exist on Earth. They showed up over 100,000,000 years ago!

an ancient scorpion trapped in amber

SPITTLEBUG

Spittlebug is the name given to the froghopper in the **nymph** stage of development. The spittlebug is an insect that makes bubbles that look like spit. (That's where it gets its name.) First, it makes a big glob of **froth**. Then, it sits inside it. That is where it grows into an adult. The froth hides the bug from predators. And those who attack the spittlebug will learn that the froth has a very bad taste.

Froghopper

spittlebug nymph

adult froghopper

Super Spit

This spittlebug's froth does more than hide the nymph. It also keeps the nymph at the right temperature and prevents the insect from drying out.

Insect Names

Spittlebugs get their name from the froth in which they hide. Many other insects get nicknames based on the way they act or look, too. There are caterpillars called *woolly bears*. Termites are sometimes called *white ants*. Fierce ants in Africa are called *army ants* or *driver ants*. Stinging ants are called *fire ants*.

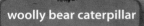
woolly bear caterpillar

An adult froghopper emerges from the froth.

BUILDING A BUBBLE

The frothy "spit" a spittlebug hides in is very important to its survival. But how does it build this bubble building?

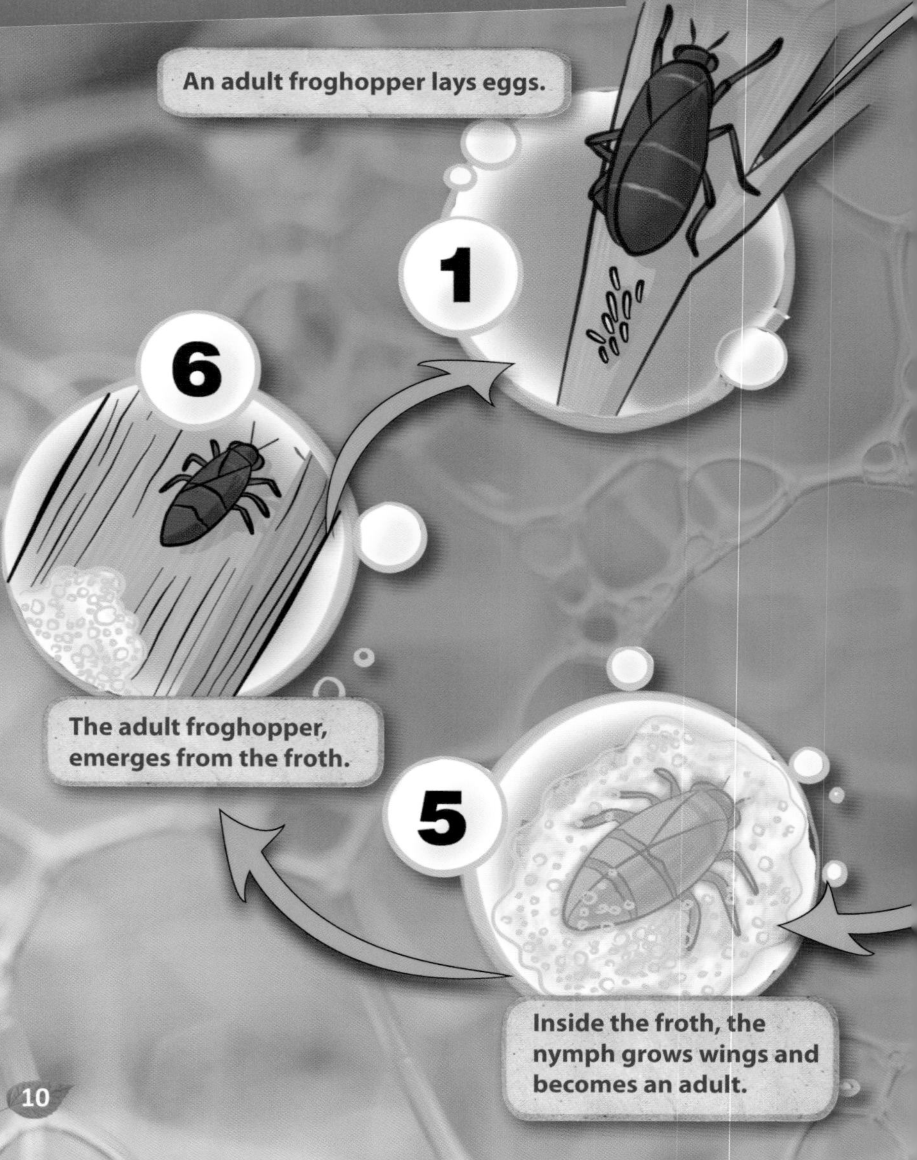

An adult froghopper lays eggs.

1

6

The adult froghopper, emerges from the froth.

5

Inside the froth, the nymph grows wings and becomes an adult.

2

In spring, the eggs hatch, and nymphs emerge.

3

The nymphs suck the sap from plants. Excess sap is forced out. Bubbles form as sap mixes with air.

4

The nymph gathers the bubbles around itself to create a hideout.

STOP! THINK...

- How do you think the spittlebug knows how much spit to produce?

- Why do you think the nymph needs extra protection?

- What kind of hideout would you design for an adult froghopper?

CADDIS FLY LARVA

The **larva** of the caddis fly lives underwater in streams. There, it builds a silk case. The case helps it catch food and protects its soft body. The larva attaches small pieces of rock, sand, or twigs to the case. The ends of the case are open. The **gills** of the larva reach out the backside for easy breathing. The legs and head stick out of the front. In the safety of its case, the larva can drag itself along the bottom of the stream.

All the rocks and twigs help it stay hidden from predators. The larva makes its case bigger as it grows. When it is ready to mature into an adult fly, it bites through the case and rises to the surface. Then it is called a *caddis fly*. But, it doesn't spend very much time flying. It normally only lives one to two weeks out of the water before it dies.

adult caddis fly

Suit of Armor

Just like the caddis fly, we protect ourselves with armor. Our armor is our clothes, shoes, jackets, and hats. We have rain jackets to keep us dry. We have shoes to protect the bottoms of our feet. We once made metal armor to protect ourselves during war.

The caddis fly moves by pulling its abdomen in and out.

The caddis fly larva uses whatever materials it can find to build its case. It may use gravel, sand, twigs, leaves or anything else nearby.

TRAPDOOR SPIDER

A trapdoor spider builds a deadly trap to catch its **prey**. This arthropod digs a hole. Then it covers it with a hidden door. The door is **camouflaged** with grass and twigs. When the spider feels something crawling above the door, it darts from its hole to attack. Carefully placed silk strands around the trap let the spider feel what's happening above the hole. The lines feed back to the spider. When a yummy bug hits one of these lines, the spider knows exactly where it is.

Trapdoor spiders hide inside their burrows. If they are very hungry, they will poke out from the trapdoor to watch and wait.

The trapdoor spider spins silk to create a hinge. This is how it attaches the door to the hole.

Hunting the Hunter

Tarantula hawk wasps specialize in hunting trapdoor spiders. They are some of the largest wasps in the world. The sting of the tarantula hawk wasp is very painful.

Down the Hatch

Human trapdoors, or hatches, are used for many reasons. They can be found in all kinds of places. In some buildings, a trapdoor leads up to a roof. On ships, hatches lead up to the higher deck. Trapdoors are sometimes used to add an element of mystery to a story.

BUILDING UNDERWATER

Some bugs live underwater and hunt for their food under the surface. Living underwater lets them hunt without competing with land bugs for food. But they still need **oxygen** to breathe. So, many bugs spend lots of time coming up for air. Some have physically **adapted** to get oxygen from the water. Other bugs build special air pockets. All of these techniques (tek-NEEKS) help them breathe underwater.

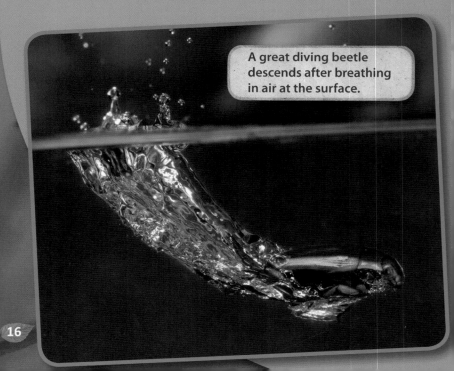

A great diving beetle descends after breathing in air at the surface.

A Breath of Fresh Air

The diving bell spider's web traps air in a bubble. The spider uses this bubble to breathe. The bubble also acts as external lungs.

GREAT DIVING BEETLE

This bug **engineer** has adapted its body to hunt and live underwater. Great diving beetles use their wing cases to collect air bubbles. This helps the beetle breathe underwater. When it has stored air, the beetle searches for food. Its favorites include other insects, tadpoles, and even small fish! When the beetle runs out of air, it swims to the surface to collect more. But don't let the name fool you. This bug not only swims and dives—it also flies.

The body of the great diving beetle is lined with dark yellow and green stripes.

great diving
beetle larva

Sometimes diving beetles eat
so much that they become too
heavy to swim.

DIVING BELL SPIDER

This spider spends its entire life underwater. Some incredible adaptations make this possible. The diving bell spider uses hairs on its body to trap a bubble of air around its abdomen. It uses this air to build an underwater web.

The web holds bubbles of air. The spider makes many trips to the surface to get more air bubbles for its web bubble. It will catch and eat almost anything that touches the underwater web.

diving bell spider

Underwater Hunters

Because the diving bell spider hunts underwater, it can catch prey that other spiders can't reach. Its prey includes aquatic insects and small fish.

Diving Helmets

Humans use diving helmets to work underwater for long periods of time. There is more pressure deep underwater than above water. The diving helmet allows divers to adjust to changes in pressure.

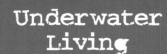

Underwater Living

Will humans one day adapt to live underwater as some bugs have? Will we grow gills somewhere on our heads, perhaps behind our ears? Marine scientist already spend time below the water studying animals, plants, and the layers of the earth. Aquanauts are people who stay underwater for long periods of time. In the future, scuba divers and submarines may not need to use oxygen tanks. And it's safe to assume, wherever humans live, we'll find bugs there, too!

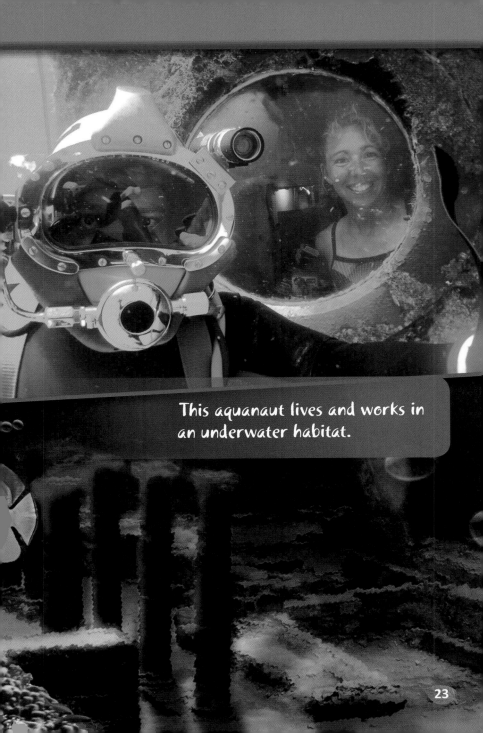

This aquanaut lives and works in an underwater habitat.

SPECIAL PROJECTS

Some bugs make structures used by thousands of insects. Others build structures that only one bug can use. Some of those buildings are **temporary** and are used for just a part of a bug's life. Other structures are used by many **generations**. The bugs don't need to be taught how to build these things. Their **instincts** tell them how. They even know how to divide up the work among thousands of bugs!

termite mound

Instincts

Instincts are a type of behavior living things use to survive. When something is coming toward your head, you don't have to think about it—you just duck! Your instincts tell you to move. Instincts also tell animals how to find food, mate, and stay safe.

wasp nest

LEAFCUTTER ANTS

Leafcutter ants are farmers. They have very sharp **mandibles**. They use them to chew plant leaves into small pieces. Then they carry the leaves to the nest. The leaves become food for a **fungus** that the ants use to feed their young.

Leafcutter ants have different jobs in the colony. Worker ants keep watch over the ants that are looking for food. These ants guard against attacks from the phorid (FOR-id) fly. The phorid fly is a **parasite**. It lays eggs on the head of the leafcutter ant. When the eggs hatch, the flies kill the ant! The smallest ant workers sometimes ride on the heads of the largest workers. Their job is to chase away phorid flies that try to land.

leafcutter ant

Fungus Farming

Leafcutter ants work hard to keep the fungus healthy. If the ants collect leaves on which the fungus will not grow, the ants will stop collecting that type of leaf. They also watch for mold and pests that may attack the fungus.

Insects have been farming fungus for millions of years. Humans began farming the land just a few thousand years ago.

SILKWORMS

Sometimes, an animal builds something so useful that even humans want to use it. Throughout history, silk has been worn by people who appreciate beautiful things. It is very smooth and soft. Silk is made by the silkworm.

The silkworm has been **domesticated** by humans. It is very rare to see a silkworm in the wild. **Sericulture** is the practice of raising silkworms to make silk. It has been done in China for more than 5,000 years.

adult silkworm moth

Each silkworm forms a cocoon that is made of one long strand of silk. Unraveled, the cocoon can stretch up to 3,000 feet.

A female silkworm can lay up to 500 eggs.

Inside a Silk Farm

The Chinese have many myths and legends about sericulture. People have been perfecting the art of making silk for thousands of years. Today, most silk is made in Japan, South Korea, and Thailand.

1.

Silk moths lay eggs on special paper.

2.

Silkworms hatch and eat mulberry leaves.

3.

Within 35 days, the caterpillar begins to spin a cocoon.

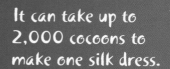

It can take up to 2,000 cocoons to make one silk dress.

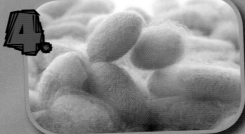

4. It takes two to three days for a caterpillar to spin itself inside the cocoon.

5. Silk farmers kill the caterpillars with heat and boil the cocoons to soften them.

6. The fibers are wound and spun into thread.

CARPENTER ANTS

Carpenter ants build their nests in wood. These ants can be found in many parts of the world. They like to make their homes in moist, dead wood. There are many parts of a house these ants will target. They like the wood around doors and windows. And they like decks. They dig tunnels with smooth walls. Little piles of sawdust make it easy to spot ant tunnels.

carpenter ants

an ant attack

Exploding Ants

Some kinds of carpenter ants explode when they're attacked. They have poison glands that explode when the abdomen contracts. The attacker is sprayed with a poisonous, sticky substance produced inside the ant's head. The ant dies, but the attacker will avoid other carpenter ants in the future!

THE FUTURE OF INSECTS

Insects may be small, but they play a big role in the environment. Imagine the world is a giant puzzle. Insects are one of the puzzle pieces. Every part works together.

Today, one of the puzzle pieces is in danger of disappearing. Bees are very important to the environment. They make honey that sweetens our food. They make the wax we use in candles and other items. But they have a more important job. Bees pollinate over 30 percent of our food crops. Without them, there would be food shortages all over the world. Scientists are working together to protect the future of bees and other insects.

Wild Robots

The next time you hear an insect buzzing close to your ear, think twice before you swat at it. You might be listening to the delicate hum of a tiny cybug—half insect, half robot! Scientists can now control the flight path of a moth by inserting a small computer in it.

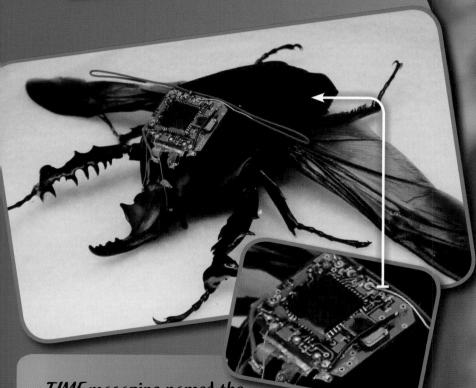

TIME magazine named the cyborg beetle one of the top 50 inventions of 2009.

BIOMIMICRY

All living creatures need protection from the weather. We need to catch or grow food to eat. We need to protect ourselves while we are sleeping. Bugs face the same challenges. Humans can learn from the way bugs solve these problems. **Biomimicry** (bahy-oh-MIM-ik-ree) is one way engineers solve problems. First, they study nature. Then, they try to find new ways to solve human problems. Biomimicry isn't about *using* nature or learning *about* nature. It's about learning *from* nature.

Airplanes were designed to mirror birds' ability to fly.

COPYCATS

Ants swarm together and attack intruders. Their behavior gave computer programmers an idea. They made a program to search computer networks for threats. What happens when a threat is found? Other programs swing into action! This is just like ants that work together to face an attacker. There are many adaptations found in nature that can help us solve our problems. This is just one of them.

Ants work together to attack intruders.

In Your Hands

Scientists and engineers use biomimicry to find what works well in nature. Join them by studying the bug builders in this book. Can you use biomimicry to come up with a new way to stay warm at night?

What about a sleeping bag inspired by the silkworm's cocoon?

Tightly-wound threads are soft and warm.

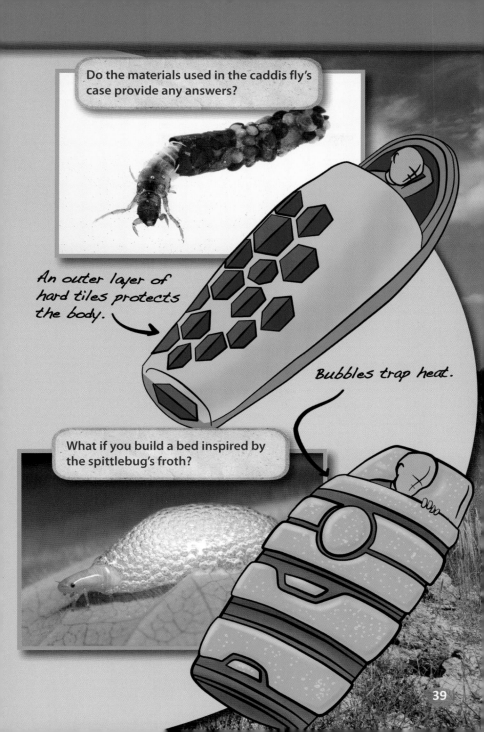

LIVING TOOLBOXES

Bug engineers have everything they need for their construction projects. Hungry insects use mandibles to chew through wood like human saws. Caddis fly larvae use rocks, sand, and wood. These materials keep the larvae safe just like a human house made of wood. Leafcutter ants build a farm the same way human farmers do. They work hard to keep their crops healthy. Insects follow their instincts to build the structures they need to survive. Like human engineers, bug builders have all the right tools and know how to get the job done.

massive mandibles

perfect pinchers

enormous eyes

all eyes on you

GLOSSARY

adapted—changed in a way that helps an organism survive in its habitat

armor—a defensive covering for the body

arthropod—an animal with three body parts, jointed limbs, and an exoskeleton

biomimicry—learning how to solve problems from animals and plants

camouflaged—colored or textured in a way that helps a plant or animal blend into its environment

domesticated—adapted to living with human beings and to serving human purposes

engineer—a person trained and skilled in designing buildings, technology, and inventions

exoskeleton—a hard protective structure on the outside of an animal's body

froth—something that is light and full of air bubbles

fungus—an organism, such as mold or mushrooms, that lives on dead or decaying matter and was formerly a plant

generations—the length of time between the birth of parents and their offspring

gills—organs used to obtain oxygen from water

instincts—natural abilities and responses

larva—a stage during the growth of an insect where it does not resemble the parent

mandibles—the mouthparts of some arthropods

nymph—a stage of an insect's growth when it resembles the parent but is smaller

oxygen—an element necessary for life that is present in the air we breathe

parasite—a living thing that lives in or on another living thing

predators—animals that kill and eat other animals

prey—animals that are consumed by others for energy

sericulture—raising silkworms to produce raw silk

skyscrapers—very tall buildings

temporary—lasting for a limited time

INDEX

BIBLIOGRAPHY

Greenaway, Theresa. *DK Big Book of Bugs*.
DK Publishing, 2000.

> Get a close-up look at a variety of different insects. Utilize text features such as the glossary and index to look up important information.

Johnson, Jinny. Simon & Schuster Children's Guide to Insects and Spiders. Simon & Schuster Children's Publishing, 1997.

> There are over 100 different insects and spiders discussed in this book. These insects and spiders are discussed in groups based on similar characteristics. Each chapter in the book discusses a different group.

Silverstein, Alvin, and Virginia B. Silverstein. *Metamorphosis: Nature's Magical Transformations*. Dover Publications, 2003.

> This book takes a look at metamorphosis by investigating the life cycles of butterflies and frogs.

Tait, Noel. *Insects & Spiders*. Simon & Schuster Books for Young Readers, 2008.

> Learn about a variety of different insects and spiders with 3-D style illustrations that make the insects and spiders in this book leap off the page!

MORE TO EXPLORE

Cirrus Image
http://www.cirrusimage.com

This website provides colorful close-up images and information about insects and spiders found in North America.

Insect Identification
http://www.insectidentification.org

The Insect Identification website provides a directory of insects and spiders that you can search by identifying key characteristics of the organism. Simply type in the primary and secondary colors, the number of legs, and the state in which you spotted the bug.

Animal Planet
http://animal.discovery.com/guides/atoz/spiders.html

The Animal Planet website has created a special page just for content on insects and spiders. You can browse the links to view information as well as videos and photos.

National Geographic for Kids
http://kids.nationalgeographic.com/kids/

National Geographic's website for kids provides information on a variety of wildlife (including insects and spiders) and provides photos and videos of wildlife from around the world, as well as games and other activities.

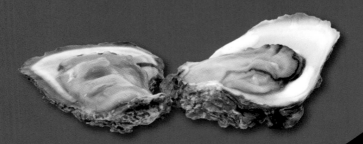

Timothy J. Bradley grew up near Boston, Massachusetts, and spent every spare minute drawing spaceships, robots, and dinosaurs. He enjoyed it so much that he started writing and illustrating books about natural history and science fiction. Timothy also worked as a toy designer for Hasbro, Inc., and designed life-size dinosaurs for museum exhibits. Timothy loves looking at bugs and the amazing things they can build.

Timothy lives in sunny Southern California with his wife and son.